# Ticking

# Ticking

by

*Ellie Rees*

First published 2022 by The Hedgehog Poetry Press

Published in the UK by
The Hedgehog Poetry Press
5, Coppack House
Churchill Avenue
Clevedon
BS21 6QW

www.hedgehogpress.co.uk

ISBN: 978-1-913499-63-1

9  8  7  6  5  4  3  2  1

A CIP Catalogue record for this book is available from the British Library.

*For my two sons, Tom and Will and my husband, Gareth*

# Contents

**House** .................................................................................................................9

Ticking.................................................................................................11
Ecdysis ...............................................................................................12
Purple .................................................................................................14
After You Died....................................................................................15
My Mother's Curtains .......................................................................16
'You have one, old message.'..............................................................17
Birdwatching......................................................................................18
Scribble ..............................................................................................19
S A D ..................................................................................................20
Grounded ...........................................................................................21
The Owl..............................................................................................24
Snowdrop............................................................................................25
Convalescing......................................................................................26


**Garden**..............................................................................................27

This Year.............................................................................................29
Spring Digging ..................................................................................30
Once Upon an April...........................................................................31
Skipping Rhyme ................................................................................32
Fox Paths ...........................................................................................34
Midsummer's Eve ..............................................................................35
The Yew Trees at Dimlands................................................................36
Apprehension.....................................................................................37
Last Pickings......................................................................................38
All Saints Day ....................................................................................39

Field .................................................................................41

Samson's Field................................................................43
'Of an age when...' ........................................................44
Conversations with Dai ................................................46
Items Found in Samson's Field ...................................48
Sheepley's Barn .............................................................50
Geometry........................................................................51
November........................................................................52
Starlings..........................................................................53
Giants..............................................................................54
Dung Spiders .................................................................55
Man with a Gun.............................................................56
Toads ...............................................................................58
Pathetic Fallacy .............................................................59


Cliffs ..............................................................................61

Disinterred.....................................................................64
Looking Back .................................................................66
The day the sea was fat.................................................67
Wedding Guest ..............................................................68
The Cliff Path ................................................................69
Nan the Lanes ...............................................................70
After Emily .....................................................................73
As if from nowhere .......................................................74
Surfers and Jumpers......................................................75
On Edge...........................................................................76
Still Life?.........................................................................77
Sheer Disbelief ..............................................................78

# HOUSE

# TICKING

Horse hooves click then panic to a clatter on
     the concrete of Huw's stable yard.

Here indoors I hear smaller tickings:
     the hanging weight in the clock on the wall;
the metal casing of the warming stove;
     and the tide clock wheezing its slow mistakes.

Listen, there are more:

the pendulum has the same rhythm as
     my heart, minute iambics beating so
in time, then the seconds – in a rush,
     caught by the vibrating minute-hand.

Inside the stove
     the logs tick
the flames lick,
     and that tide clock needs resetting.


Outside, great tits chant their trochees.

# ECDYSIS

The weight of January's leaden light,
the patient wait for the days to lengthen;

should I shed my skin and begin again
shining and wet in anticipation?

Rub as I might I can't clear a thin film
that clings to my eyes, confuses my sight.

It's enough to meander on like this,
too cold for some reincarnation...

No. Need to slough off what adheres so fast,
the past with all its detritus.

I'll no longer ignore cardboard boxes,
fruiting bodies infesting my loft;

they have spored generations of attics
and rendered the dead down to this:

ashtrays, empty frames, an odd napkin ring,
a metal box full of threepenny-bits, keys,

locked up in their own corrosion,
just an encumbrance of pewter and brass.

One box seems empty, light as a puffball,
whispers of something concealed inside:

a heap of transparencies, Kodak slides,
gossamer wisps in coloured disarray.

'View from this side'. I hold one to the light,
the years slip like silken scales from my eyes.

Embroidered with dust, the past is re-dressed:
the house where I lived, *look* – long derelict,

it's resurrected in a setting sun,
all its lost windows open to the heat.

January simply cannot compete
or compare with these glittering cast-offs.

Here I am, wading through opalescence,
child-Aphrodite in blue, rubber swim-hat.

I'm bewitched by the skin I once lived in.

# PURPLE

I knew I was dreaming: roaming well-loved rooms,
the gloom of the evening, even the street's orange lights
might have prompted a persuasion of reality;
I knew I was dreaming nevertheless –
unless my senses were to be believed?
I breathed the polished floors of my childhood home,
thrown by their honest solidity.
The rug's purple thread felt no premonition
or dread, caressing the soles of my feet.
Completely awake, a memory stirred – I recalled
scarlet birds had embroidered the walls –
and so their colours sang as I ran from room to hall.
But again I was roused to remember, this house
was now rubble, a builder's back yard.

Time thickens, the hour hand stumbles.

The vision stayed hidden, forgotten
for a while, until with a sort of
smile, I remembered:
my home never had wooden floors,
scarlet song never rang from those walls.
No purple carpet ever unfurled
beneath
my halting steps.

# AFTER YOU DIED

For just a few days, after you died,
as I entered the house
I'd call out to you –
'It's only me.'

I didn't expect a reply,
but you were still there,
asleep in your chair –
or playing hide-and-seek
maybe.

I no longer hear
your footstep on the stair.
Sometimes I think
it's more than I can bear.

# MY MOTHER'S CURTAINS

They don't hang well, and they smell –
not of my childhood as I'd dreamed
(I refused to have them cleaned)
but just of age and the years bundled
under the spare bed where my father slept.
They hung once in a house full of smokers
which accounts for their jaundiced pallor;
they need to fade to ivory once more,
recover their memory of colour.

This year the Spring has declined to
come for her, one more time.
She has forgotten that she ever was
and what she read and what she knew.
I've sold all her books about Gladstone,
Disraeli, Dawkins, the Papacy,
box-sets of Bruckner meant as a legacy,
vinyl, cassettes in need of conversion.
I only wanted her curtains.

At the hem, I discover
her stitching – like a genetic code.
I need to alter her adaptations:
the cotton is rotting, easy to break;
I pull out her threads, then remember the white hair
I brushed from her black cashmere jumper
the day that I bagged it for charity,
the day I hung on to her curtains.

## 'YOU HAVE ONE, OLD MESSAGE.'

I've just pressed that button again
accidentally – and there you are.
From all your long years
this moment is selected,
pre-set in a handset;

perhaps I'll decide to delete you.

You must have shivered.
      Someone walk over your grave?
Did the sunlight quiver?
You really didn't mean it
as your *dernier cri...*
You weren't even talking to me.

'Is that you Diana?  Yes, lovely –
I'll see you soon,'

is all that I'm left with.
I didn't even get to choose.

*'You have no more messages.'*

# BIRDWATCHING

This is what old people do:
birds come to them, show
their ordinary mysteries.

We have time to watch them,
share their consequence.

All day
five swallow fledglings have
teetered on the railing outside my window,
preening,
feeding.
The wind hurls the adults in swirls,
shuffles the young, like a corps de ballet
in tandem along the rail.
Their down is sculpted, pared by the wind,
then one of them
stretches a perfect wing.
A parent swoops in and they shimmy –
scattering flakes of light.

I rescue a fledgling
flown into the house:
throw a tea towel over it,
pick up – so gently – this puff of life,
then open the towel outside.

It rides the wind over the roof.

A sparrowhawk flies straight at me,
its feet clasping a shrieking swallow –
like a mother running with a child in a pushchair.

# SCRIBBLE

My hand and pen have fallen out.
The flow of thought from brain to paper
   no longer travels
with hand's consent.

I've lost my grip:
something has nobbled my fingers

and the nib
now plays *diminuendo*
                feeling its way across the page.

How loose, how easy the keyboard:
a mere touch will elicit
surrender
and words come –
with promiscuous pleasure.

But there was something, surely romantic
in the kiss of a pencil on parchment,
the cushion of my palm caressing its face,
my pride in forming elegant letters;
such confident consonants, the swirl of my vowels.

The keyboard proffers
plastic wafers
like after-dinner mints,
a postprandial game of Scrabble
perhaps?

# S A D

It seemed to be February. I started to read poems about this month, where the bleakness was soldered onto the paper. And then I looked at my screen and saw it was the last day of January. Still January.

It's anything but still, outside: once again the wind is thrashing the black yews; the bays sway and the stiff grey cherry will surely snap if it does not learn to flex. Lead and slate: the garage roof, as I look down from this upstairs window, is indeed slate and its colour has leached into the rain-soaked limestone of the walls. The skeleton of a hawthorn scratches at the sky. On the horizon the sea exhibits a paler shade of lead, whipped into turbulence. Lead – Pb – reminiscent of plums somehow, or am I thinking plumb lines? Lines of squalls are wind-dragged up the channel. There are plums as dark as this winter but this day lacks their iridescence.

Beyond the garden wall: the only true colour the monochrome green of the fields, though there are hints of yellow where the vegetation has drowned and now rots. Yellow lilies and roses in a vase on the windowsill; even though they are dying, their colour is still so bright that it hurts my eye and I turn away.

# GROUNDED

From my desk,
six horizons:
sky, Somerset, sea,
far field,
meadow, then lawn,
swallow-stitched together.

*

Upstairs, there's laughter on the radio,
a comic entertains empty rooms.
Downstairs I doodle blank pages while
wet dogs
snooze.
Across the hall, my son's wheelchair creaks
as he heaves himself onto his bed.

The trees
breathe.

*

At first a still focus
on the lawn
blackbird is subject to

gravity

then a flurry
a fuss of wings
a shimmering reappearance
closer

his tail flutes upwards
and
(gymnast)
he regains balance.

*

21

A sudden cannonade of birds outside.
Exploded out of the kitchen
I'm in the ring, can smell the sawdust, see
Red Indian tail feathers,
a clown's yellow stockings,
the swallows trapezing their outrage.

Manipulating its prey as it flies,
a silhouette – dark puppeteer –
careers towards the yew's canopy.
Sparrowhawk.

\*

Flummeries of pigeons
bully through trees
as I study the heat-warped sky.
A lone bluebottle fumbles at a window.
Above
a mewling buzzard laments its solitude.
Only swallows defy the heat's weight
weaving the loom of horizons,
shuttling between the wefts of the wind,
finding no resistance.

\*

Once I dreamed I'd found the secret of flight
but they demanded a demonstration,
proof.
So, I showed them.
Soaring above the rose-covered arches
I looked down –
their open mouths were crimson flowers.

Now turned to stone
I orbit my sun.

The pull of his gravity
allows illusions
of escape

though only
elliptical.

# THE OWL

I heard no feathered thud
no hoot nor shriek
nor muffled snap
no tell-tale puff of owl-debris.
It left a lasting impression though
a realist portrait painted in dust
each feather, filament stencilled on glass
but its head was merely a smudge.
So burnished by the October sun
it appeared a sacred icon,
a gift for the house, a fingerprint
from another dimension.

At Goldcliff on the Severn Estuary
footprints of a human family
are stratified in estuarine silts and peat.
Their walk, six thousand years ago
now seems just as ephemeral
as the delicacy of wings outstretched
each feather attuned to night's quiet air
that moment of open-winged surprise,
casually
                snapped by my window pane.

# SNOWDROP

Waiting for another diagnosis
in this dead time of the year –
I study a snowdrop, picked for this purpose.
I'm trying to pin it down with words, but
in the end
I draw it.
There's a lingering smell of honey.
My attention is caught by a fly
buzzing on the inside of my window.
If I let it out it won't last long,
better a bitter, soaring moment?
I know what I am doing with this snowdrop –
it fails to console.
Still, there is that memory of honey.

# CONVALESCING

In summer I dare to look north,
still see the sun as it sets
touching the room with light.
I gaze each night
as it dips
in new places
behind trees I meant to visit –

behind trees I mean to visit.

Then I stop watching:
try to forget
the light retreating,
the poppies too heavy to hold up their heads;
the birds – water-weighted – have gone to ground.
Except for the swallows –
except for the martins coaxing their young
away from the nests
under the eaves of the north-facing room.

Lying in bed I watch.
Like a pack of cards tossed in the wind
they explode outside the window.
The white of the sky like the white on their backs,
like the walls of this room.

When did I realise my summers were countable?

# GARDEN

# THIS YEAR

For the first time in months the sun is warm upon my back as I bend over the ruined flowerbeds. Sticks, dead leaves, empty snail shells mask the tips of forgotten alliums planted on my birthday. This year, there is no strength in my fingers to pull out the weeds, and the secateurs hurt. An old woman – the one I am becoming – keeps pestering me. I thought ageing would be a gradual process, didn't realise it would progress in leaps. This leaping is the only lithe thing about me. Come July, she hasn't quite gone away and I ponder the merits of a straw hat as I stand upright and stretch. Summer is a hiatus, the crest of a wave that can be surfed until September; then the long struggle not to drown. I stoop and blow on a bumblebee, spread-eagled in shameless ecstasy, making love to the centre of a dahlia. Still alive!

# SPRING DIGGING

No firm footing, a spongy resistance
like a dream of trampling corpses.
Bulbs – small skulls
on a slab of soil
ready for dissection.
Something
has been tunnelling.

Not moles – there is no spill,
but a careful digger,
something weasely;
now I'm thinking rats,
sappers with a vast ambition,
ready to gorge
on all that is buried
long before it flowers.

How deep do they go?
The holes I mean,
slack mouths drooling;
mortuaries for snails –
slug nests –
deep throats lined with all that is slime.

# ONCE UPON AN APRIL

Had a luminous hula-hoop once.
Could flex my trunk just like a young tree
and watch as the hoop swirled around me.
Rooted, I swayed my body again
heard a green song spiral about me,
never to fall at my feet;
nonchalantly chewing bubble gum
I blew such shocking pink bubbles.

Cherry-blossom pink as Candy Floss
whisked around a stick,
an effervescence of sticky sweetness
frilled with fairground excitement.

Had a magic paint-book too.
Remember those banks of flowers and shrubs
drawn in the shape of lollipops?
A paintbrush dipped in a glass of water
could caress each blob into life –
though of a synthetic colour.
Now, April's rain fills the empty spaces,
brushing the trees a fluorescent green.

The lace and frills of my tree-peony flower –
the colour of my very first lipstick.
Oh how, aged twelve, I desired its iridescence
purchased in Woolworths – illicitly.

# SKIPPING RHYME

Cowslip, buttercup, celandine and dandelion –
buttercup, dandelion, cowslip and celandine.

*(You are in!)*

GOLD is their colour but their
shimmers aren't the same –
glossy is the celandine,

*(Skip in a line!)*

Freshly painted buttercup,

*(All jump up!)*

Cowslip's flower case –
a papery lime.
Silly is the celandine,
eight petals splayed,

*(Six, seven eight!)*

stamens lean away
from its green ovary.
Humble are the buttercup's
overlapping petals,

*(Three, four, five!)*

stamens curved protectively
around a hidden womb.
Three-coloured celandine:
green, yellow, gold –
calyx split in three:

*(One, two three!)*

Buttercup with green sepals,
one for every petal,
sepal of the celandine
so fine you can ignore it.
Cowslip, cowslip,
how many florets?

*(One two three four,
five and six!)*

32

Each flower spat from
its green CAL-YX!
But
what about the dandelion?

*(You are OUT!)*

# FOX PATHS

This year the brothers do not want our hay,
all their cattle were spirited away
in a slurry of cruel allegations:
'A harrowing case of wilful neglect.'

Midsummer's day and machinery pulses,
neighbouring hay fields are swirled and dried,
but here, Burnet moths display
scarlet spots – they flick their wings, unperturbed.

Fox-shaped furrows in the grass flanked with musk
give way to flattened places in our meadow.
The grasses are dull, heavy-headed with seed
but the trampled secret places glimmer.

Foxes take short-cuts, know to cut corners,
they've made this hidden hole in the hedge.
Here one must have rested, waited, then pounced:
still, an explosion of fur stalks the air.

A squall sweeps in – the fox paths decay,
new places in the grass, not animal at all:
elemental whorls with no trace of fox –
it's as if they've been blown away.

Huw Jones wants to see where his house martins nested,
heaves himself over our wall.
Neighbourly, he offers to take all our hay:
'There's plenty of time even now,' he says –

adds, 'That damn fox been taking my gleanies,
had four of them shot just last week.'
*Knew* I'd heard gunshot on the wind that day,
wind that wiped the foxes' secrets away.

# MIDSUMMER'S EVE

Then there is a moment of entering into another's world. Bending over the flowerbed to pull out a thistle, a foxglove brushes my face. Inside the petal I hear legs rasping: a bumblebee so close, it is inside my brain. Swallows and martins swirl above and around me, and so – maestro – I conduct, waving my arms in the air. The swallows fly with their first brood; the martins still feed their young. On the shed roof a solitary blackbird taps out a persistent, low-key alarm call. A horse splutters – it echoes – and from the far trees, unseasonably, the tinny drumming of a woodpecker. 8pm on a perfect midsummer's evening. The sun is still as high as a winter's noon and dazzles the lupins, the bruised delphiniums, though the poppies seem merely dazed. No sound other than the birds and the horse and the distant bleat of a train. Still bright at 10pm: a single thrush, and the sunset. Stray wisps of pink fanfare the sky. At night, with the window open, I can hear the murmuring of the martins in their nests. 4am and it all begins again.

# THE YEW TREES AT DIMLANDS

Not planted to frame the view from my house
not meant for me to measure
the rise and fall of the silver tide
though the Severn still threads them together.

Like scattered parts of a 'heritage' jigsaw
whose central piece has been long mislaid –
redundant since Dimlands House burned down
the yews have forgotten their function.

Instead of composing what I should see
these trees have intervened –
an interruption between the sea and my house
a picture that's oddly askew.

Rusty, singed, their pollen like sulphur
already dead at the top –
their shadows still fall on grassy hollows
the gaps   in the old kitchen-garden wall.

# APPREHENSION

*'Will you go hunt, my lord?'*

*Twelfth Night*

Butterflies
tumble in the warming air,

flying-ants swarm,
twisting like smoke.

There's only the click
of the swallows' beaks as they swoop

then whirl around my feet,
and the purr of clover-drugged bees.

And then comes that throat-torn, fear-born wail;

it has a dying
fall.

It sweeps across the garden,
shreds the quiet air:

a mammal or a bird carried back
towards the cliffs,
back to a precipitous nest.

If insect apprehension could be heard,
what horror...

# LAST PICKINGS

I coaxed these tendrils clock-wise
around each stick, secured them with string;
now the vine's once-youthful winding
nakedly exposed, is stiffer than twine.

Elsewhere so much leaf, concealing
arthritic hands of beans, their fingers
stung by a first hint of frost.
Woozy flies bask on papery leaves.

What's left to glean on this shining day?

Slug-split carrots with matted feathers
fingers of squash dead at their tips
vertiginous lettuces, triffid chard
chives fat as pencils, purple topped.

This slant-eyed sun reveals
gleaming sediment – silver debris:
ropes of cobweb spiralling their riders,
stray wisps of hair, an insect's wing.

Motionless, I watch everything move:

dust motes dance with midges,
golden spiders spasm;
a single feather cruises past
as ponderous as a whale.

# ALL SAINTS DAY

We wake to altered horizons,
        until the sun
                breaks through the mist
and trees rise
        like rusty shipwrecks at low tide
                trimmed by a ribbon of gulls.

Surprised by light, this house
        is an island.
                Only the pulse
of a distant foghorn
        swells through the watery
                silence.

We open the door:
        two geese sway towards us,
                side by side splashing
through copper leaves.
        They open their wings –
                an angelic challenge
white feathers dazzle –
        then daunted
                they turn their heads away.

The garden is a riot of indecision:
        nasturtiums clamber through
                purple cosmos;
late roses trapped
        in mud-spattered bud;
                sweet peas – mere tissue paper.

A lazy warmth; the air is thick, shining
        with insect husks,
                a wren makes ripples in the stillness.
Mist sinks like dust
        between the sea and the window
                and now the light dies early.

# FIELD

# SAMSON'S FIELD

Idly watching haymaking in our meadow I'm jostled by a field of rapeseed on the other side of Dimlands Road. Its feathered seed-heads are the colour of bone and crackle with malice. At root, this posturing conceals the bald earth, scabby with stones. I prefer it when, a chemical yellow, its flowers shriek at the blue of the sky and stain me, waist-high. Thistles explode: tufts of fluff drift; butterflies flicker between the bindweed. The larks are silent, bested by pigeons that flap like gunshot then wheeze away. This field's the colour of an old pub wall; the rapeseed coughs a last death rattle.

When the swallows leave and cease to distract, I stand at an upstairs window staring south. My line of sight crosses the road, swoops over the naked fields to the sea, and is finally arrested by the top of Exmoor. It tethers a landscape that otherwise, threatens to peel away. Walking along the footpath that crosses Samson's Field, I stumble across my sight line; it stops me in my tracks. I turn to see its origin, my window in the distance. Am I here in this field, or seeing it from over there? The gulls soar then drift – they seem unfettered – but the footpath hesitates; its muddy footprints turn aside. Perhaps they are mine?

# 'OF AN AGE WHEN...'

*After 'Snowy Egret' by Robert Hass*

A woman *walks out in the morning with a* bowl.
Damp air, grey skies, wind from the west
and the distant surf drumming Nash Sands.
The wind plays music with the stops
in the dovecot, dances round the Tythe Barn;
trees in Abbots Ley squeak and groan,
nuzzling each other for comfort.
Last night she had feared they would fall
on her roof. She *is of an age* that expects
disaster, she thinks that this thought
was sent to upbraid her for thinking
how happy she'd be if Billy were beside her –
and not in that brig, dragged by the tide,
backwards towards Nash Sands.
She *is of an age* that's put aside its courage,
no longer to dream of a better
day, though endurance is not the word
that she utters. This morning she chooses
to walk up Slutts Lane: clutching the bowl
under her apron will warm her stiff fingers.
Her boots slip and fumble
in icy ridges, yesterday's walking, frozen in mud.
The lane ducks down below the hedges,
there's a taste of iron in the thickening air.
Frost-covered grasses fringing the path
peck at her skirt, she's snagged by dead brambles.
Rooks rise and squabble, clatter above her:
she hears Wathan Wood is near, knows
to avoid its abandoned quarry,
just feels herself blindly along Slutts Lane.
The west wind carries the creak of harness,
the smell of tobacco, a stink of horse piss.
A woman walking out in the morning with a bowl.
A man on a horse of an age to be kind.

'Where be thee going, Peggy?' leaning down.
'I be going to Sheepley's barn with Billy's dinner.'
'And what have thee got for his dinner, Peggy?'
'Mashed taters, skimmed milk,' she replies.
'What be he doing there now, Peggy?'
'Why, threshing sir, he told me, when he left.'
'Ah – take my rein, Peggy, I'll be your eyes.
I know Billy's gone, but you'll come to no harm.'

# CONVERSATIONS WITH DAI

No two masons will do the same work,
me and Rhodri swapped ends – mix and match –
the wall, the stonework then looked just the same.
There's an awful lot of fireplaces, chimneys and walls
yes, all of the older properties.
Stone picking? We did it when we were kids,
just piled them in the back of a trailer,
it put a few bob in your pocket.

We don't plough as deep today as we used to,
nine inches and you'd hit all the pin rock.
The big pieces – they'd be the ones used for walls,
the rest would be dumped in a corner.
I was taught by my uncles, their uncle
taught them – I wonder how far back it goes?
Stones lay in wait for me even then
though I thought I would be a carpenter.

It's everything really, though I have to
spread out – I worked for the diocese of Llandaff.
See this hole in the wall where the stone has crumbled?
It's more like a gap.
That stone was sacrificial – no, not like that!
This wall's not old; they might have used cement
so the moisture seeped into the stone.
It shaled and became sacrificial.

I'm fortunate to work with lime mortar,
use this, it's softer, absorbs all the water,
lime mortar becomes sacrificial instead.
Some stones will peel, put the wrong way up,
up on end they will often start shaling;
you can see there's a flaw soon after it rains,
it stays grey when the rest starts to dry;
you develop an eye for a grain after time.

Or maybe the boulder that filled this gap
had fissures which made it unstable.
You can tell after time just by looking, but
hit with a hammer it rings like a bell,
fissures not fossils make a deader sound.
If flawed and laid just as it was formed
the weight of the wall stops it fracturing.
Stonewalls repair themselves; lime makes amends.

I'm not against cement, not all of the time
but not on an old house – keep it as it was.

# ITEMS FOUND IN SAMSON'S FIELD

*Buried beneath the plough-raked limestone:*

eight gold Roman coins
    one golden ring
two silver Tudor groats
    a single silver thimble
a US Air Force silver cap badge
    a copper Victorian Penny
in bronze, an awl and
    two axe heads
a Chinese good luck charm

and half a tile
    made of marble

Not white not pure
    not Michelangelo
just one dimension
    with rust in its veins
shaved from a block of greys

*Buried inside the tile:*

A Roman matron
    a garland in her hair
an image of ancient mintage
    a forgotten Empress
or a plebeian face etched upon a sarcophagus

Her mouth forms the eye
    of a lion now emerging
her eyelid the chin of a child
    who is hiding
half-smiling in the curls of her hair

The lion's other eye
        now a leering mouth
in a face with no skin
        it looks over her shoulder
she does not feel its breath on her cheek

*On the surface a raised relief-map:* a white plastic broom head with blue
nylon bristles

# SHEEPLEY'S BARN

The barn recalls the fallen walls,
truncated pillars of ancient abbeys,
its congregation only sheep
its plainsong that of gulls.
It is unoffended by the lichen
graffitied on its stones,
like medieval paintings
of leering demon eyes.

A place where now few verticals
dissect the fallen rubble,
they were worked by a master
craftsman, his edges sharp
his corners true.
Two of the windows still clearly defined,
lined with cut stone, are brim-full of sky;
cock-and-hen capstones strut on clean slate,
but the wind has taken the mortar.

A managed collapse: such a tidy ruin,
not one stray boulder, not a slate from its roof –
nettles thrust through its tumbled walls,
yet someone has poisoned the thistles,
put metal gates to patch some of the gaps
though nothing is being kept out, or in –
listen to the wind running through it!

# GEOMETRY

I resist these rows of summer stubble,
weave instead a drunken path,
wander the edges.

Dawdle through flotsam
of last year's rapeseed, another year's barley,
the stunted wheat.

My feet are kneaded by limestone rubble,
above, dying vapour-trails
furrow the sky.

Cross-hatching the rows, new tractor tracks
point where the straw bales stood;
a remaining stook still leans askew.

Ambling through this field of geometry,
my shadow bisects each track that I take:
I look up – the horizon arcs.

Horse dung steams in the quiet air.
I think it almost seems to be singing
it rises in such exultation

defying the parallel lines.

# NOVEMBER

Ten days of rain and the footpath has become a tidal causeway. Just off the sodden track in a corner of Samson's field is a shrine to stone – a heap of rain-washed rubble. Spring ploughing agitates the pin rock but the stones rise in silence in the autumn – each morning more appear, stony fungi, spored by the rain. Straw manikins, voodoo dolls left by rape roots, are dissolving now, losing their colour-kinship with the stones. Sea and sky are the colour of limestone, bitter as salt. Only land-locked gulls are paler, and the tips of the breakers, heaving in from the Atlantic. A buzzard's cry rebounds from the rock. The horizon crept even closer last night and merged the sky and the sea with Somerset on the other side, just a blur of grey. Hedges and woodland have mulched down to brown and the rain has tamed the wind; the sodden air droops like yesterday's washing left out too long. A solitary crow stabs at bloated apples and the gutters' rain-drenched music is choked with moss.

# STARLINGS

My feet already in shadow,
I skip a splash of feathers
and what remains
of a breastbone,
clean as a plastic toy;

its edges transparent, already dissolving
melting into the grass.

The air thickens, I can smell
the frost, watch a red sun fall
behind far trees.

A sycamore rings with metallic
chatter: starlings –
their voices honed by the cold.

Now there's black movement in the sky.

# GIANTS

In this country of many horizons:
fields edged by sea, then Somerset and sky
only Wathan Wood intersects.
Within, five fallen giants
have yanked what was hidden, erect:
a sliced root map
a primitive rood-screen
the trees' secret tracery of their seeking
sustenance, stability, the vertical.
Their bleached geometry suggests
mammoth foreheads, thrusting tusks,
honey-comb fungi where their mouths should be.

Two fields away the footpath wavers:
at Dimhole, ghosts still germinate.
Here a mighty fish was cast ashore
more than six-hundred years ago.
'The stench from its putrid carcass
led to maladies near and far
so the local people burned it
spreading sickness to man and beast.
Sir Edward Stradling gave cows to the poor.'

On Dimhole shore a driftwood fire
has left wet ashes mixed with debris
from a fisherman's late-night burger.
Lifted, winnowed by a tide-born breeze
they scour the cliff face, scurry into caves,
drift along the footpath towards Wathan Wood.

The trees in Wathan Wood now grow red sores,
reminiscent of sea-anemones.

# DUNG SPIDERS

Huw Jones has mucked out his stables.
All day his tractor smokes past the house,
tips another dump in Samson's field,
builds a steaming barrow – nothing buried here,
save the petrified roots of rapeseed.
Mounds of dung and straw
smoulder, whisper to the raw, autumn air.

So why days later
does he cover it in plastic –
strands of fine-spun polythene
draped like a veil?
Gift-wrapped in cling-film
to enhance a heap of dung.

Archaic words like *gossamer*
play in my eye's mind;
there's movement
in this failing light:
spider-brides, beneath the veil.

Smoke turns to flame: the heap combusts.
From the shelter of a darkened window
I watch its fireflies dance.
Next day there's blackened straw, scorched craters,
a Vesuvius glow –
no spider spinners,
no poultice of snow.

Heat evaporates; all the muck is spread,
but amongst its undigested gobbets,
Huw Jones must have scattered
patches of lace...

Beneath each one hides a spider-wife,
nurtured by manure – wedded to dung.

# MAN WITH A GUN

It's the oddity of the planting I recall:
the field of fodder beet squeaking underfoot,
gnarled tubers heaved beneath the leaves;
weeds tall as you – looming scarecrows
straddled the waves of a vegetable sea.
And then there was the maize.

You don't remember the beet at all,
instead it's the maize, the way that we laughed
as it whispered hoarsely above our heads.
We raised our elbows in self-defence,
corralled in circles to wander its tunnels,
scratched by erect, ginger-whiskered cobs.

You led the way, you found an opening
fringed with nettles, to a rapeseed field.
Harvested already, the skeletal stalks
jutted like spears in an ancient myth.
Our walking flushed pigeons – with a slap
and a bang – a heavy buzzard followed

and as we turned the corner of a wood
there in the distance –
a man with a gun.

I would have turned round if I'd been alone
but then you hailed him, in a masculine way,
full of frank fellowship, farming know-how.

Later you talked of the age of the gun,
its fine chased-metalwork above the trigger,
a family heirloom, older than him.
I just noticed he was tied up with string:
his belt, boot laces, the stock of his gun,
his tongue as well for all he would say.

After we parted I kept looking back
afraid we were still in his sights.
He stood there – sullen – in a crack of light.

# TOADS

I blundered
upon a troop of toads:

not a knot; not one
wore another like a rucksack –
they seemed to be quite self-contained.

Arrested, alert
they faced away from me:
their backs such a vibrant burnt-orange;
I could see their spines and the warts,
a synchronicity on the lawn.

There must have been twenty, there might have been more.

Where were they going and why had they stopped?

        Dead leaves from the beech tree, frisked by the wind

        landing upright –
        an identical tilt

        stalk-end half-buried
        in the clumps of grass –

or maybe the worms
were pulling them down

down underground
already.

# PATHETIC FALLACY

It is slow walking around Sampson's Field with boots squeaking into the mud. The tips of the hedges have been flayed by the cold. Knots of ivy have wrestled two trees to the ground and skinned the bark from another. Its peeled trunk shines nakedly, robes of bark and ivy dishevelled at its foot. The day glitters; there's yellow gorse on the top of a hedge. I hide the low sun behind the oak but the skylarks hide themselves in front of it. I can't tell if they are in the air or singing at my feet; when I stop walking, they stop singing.

I blink away my tears.

Shining white it stands upright where yesterday it wasn't. A limestone splinter, a plastic bag? I squint and shade my eyes. Curved neck, head turned away, it doesn't move when I clap my hands but then something shifts inside my head. Shining on rainwater in a furrow, the sun has made what was flat, erect. I want to believe – to say – to laugh: the sun has imagined a heron! But I am the only one imagining this field.

# CLIFFS

Limestone cliffs
vertical
soaring
through time
descending
layer
upon
layer
limestone platforms

limestone cliffs

limestone    platforms
lay      er
up      on
lay      er
ascen      ding
through    time
soar    ing
verti    cal
lime    stone

# DISINTERRED

*'800-year-old monk found sticking out of cliff face'* (Express, March 11th 2014)

The dead don't usually stand out like this.
   His legs, poking through the cliff face,
      look like a pair of over-flow pipes
         installed by deluded plumbers.

In almost any other edifice
      you'd guess them to be man-made
         efficiently flushing the water away –
            instead, they are made of man.

Beneath them, hidden in the cliff's fresh scree,
      the knees and all that remains of the legs.
         A sailor, buried, feet facing the sea
            and the waves that today are breaking.

Nash Sands would have broken his boat, and him.
   Now the sea is reclaiming him – foot by foot.

Or maybe a monk, whose habit brushed stone floors,
      whose sandaled feet often felt the kiss of the rain.
         His knees would be calloused with prayer and hard
labour,
            he was young when he died, he'd know how
to dance.

A Monknash burial seems almost poetic
      (the monastery now is as ruined as him)
         a monk, or a sailor, or both perhaps;
            he would have had an immortal soul.

Did these bones benefit from Christian burial
     or foreigner, was he denied his last rites?
          *Remember man that thou art dust*
               *and to dust, one day, thou must return.*

His bones will end as sand, not dust,
     Bewitched by the sea into coral and pearls.[1]

---

[1] But it wasn't his knees, legs and feet
that fell –
(he'd been buried the other way round).
When the cliff seemed to hold
his animal parts
I imagined him merely disabled.
This new discovery calls all in doubt:
he's 'all in pieces, all coherence gone'
the shell of his skull
strewn over the beach
cardboard-boxed to await carbon dating.

# LOOKING BACK

It's a frontier of sorts, this cliff-backed shoreline:
all of the houses face the same way.
I look at the sea all day.

From wherever I stare the view is the same:
a single fishing boat for daily hire
plays at something forgotten now.

A rusty dredger nudges Nash Sands,
a Japanese carrier swings on its anchor then
loiters drunkenly for the next high tide.

Only at night am I truly awake as my pulse
responds to a helicopter's throb;
my eyes are drawn to the opposite shore where
flashing red beacons warn of a wreck.

A child, I stood on the other side
still looking at the sea, these cliffs invisible
from over there, just a smudge on a dull horizon.

There was sand, not shale beneath my bare feet
when I ran, skipping over the worm casts
and all of the time the sand dunes whispered

and the tide was always coming in
though it teased with its small hesitations.
All the shells sang as they
slipped through my hands.

# THE DAY THE SEA WAS FAT

Today, tide and wind and low pressure have made the sea look different somehow, as if it has breathed out and elbowed more room between the two bluffs of St Donat's bay. Down at the seafront, at a safe distance behind the sea wall, I listen to the growl of boulders the size of small cars, as the water rumbles them back down the slipway. There's a fluttering inside me, like the quickening of an unborn child. I move my hand protectively to my stomach as the earth's vibrations travel to the soft core of my gut. At a distance there is a constant roar, but closer, the thump and thwack of particular waves as they smack into the cliffs on either side – a pause, then the rush of the spray as it hits the sea wall. The hiss of racing foam surges up the slipway and fingers its way under closed doors, into the lifeboat station. The cliffs ring like a cracked bell. I have never felt so alive.

# WEDDING GUEST

They did not see her shining,
the three boys on a rock-strewn beach;
they sat, facing me, on a washed-up branch,
staring at the sea;
they did not see the bride
being photographed behind them.

I was the uninvited guest –
I watched her over their heads –
and oh,

her veil was snagged by sunlight,
her body, curved bronze beneath.
Foam lay like lace on the incoming tide,
as the bride still posed on the slipway.
She glowed like a ghost in the daytime,

her groom – suggestive of nothing
save angles – half-hidden
in a shadow thrown by the cliffs.

I'll be that indistinct silhouette,
blessing or cursing in the background,
I'll be there waiting
                                    when
her wedding pictures come.

# THE CLIFF PATH

That walk belongs to tomorrow.
I'll put it off
again.

I tell myself the path is rough,
the mud so treacherous.
Roots that jut – just to trip me,
my boots not up to the job.

Like a stuck wet leaf,
vertigo will clamp me,
fixed at a tilt
away from the edge.

And a stick belongs to tomorrow as well.

# NAN THE LANES

*("The Ancient Town of my Birth": Recollections of Llantwit Major from Illtyd Thomas, collected by his daughter Marie Trevelyan in 1894)*

Miss Anne Rees known as Nan the Lanes
was much respected by the gentry
and local people generally.
She imposed on her scholars
(interspersed with good manners)
the rudiments of education.
She wrote a very fine hand,

*Is that all?*

and lived to a good old age.

*Is that all? My lips are numb - my eyes still dream*
*        I am crossing Swine Bridge over*
*Ogney's Stream        now*
*I am waiting        at Samson's Well        where am I really        who can tell*
*should I pause        for a while        in Burial Lane        It seems I must*
*be her again*

*        Someone is recalling me waking me*
*                        making me*
*                        up*

I walk over her grave very often
with reverence for her dust,
that casket once contained the body
that taught me my A B C.

*I remember... atomies        I ... an atomy*
*naked bones now dust*
*shaken*

The boys of the town frequented her orchard
to throw her fruit and nuts to the ground,
but her old dog knew them
and the boys knew him,
she was powerless
to get them down from the trees.

*I look up to the trees I see faces of boys through the leaves*
*I know them all by name they lie close to me now*
*names written on stone they have forgotten*
*they called to me*
*they call to me with no shame*

They'd cry out at the top of their voices,
'Cuckoo' to vex her the more.

*naked bones now dust*
*awakened by the wind*
*high above the lanes*
*flying*

Prior to her death,
she had her old mastiff
hanged from the gatepost
then buried in the orchard, decently
fearing it would be mistreated.
She died not long after, herself.

*Myself... my self*
*so much forgotten*
*myself*
*misbegotten*
*reborn in an old man's memory*

*I will dream again along the cliff paths of this coast*
*where grey waves tumble*
*where boulders rumble*
*with a deep Atlantic growl.*
*In winter, the low sun will dazzle me,*
*in summer reflecting off the sea –*
            *it will pare my eyes like an over-ripe fruit –*

*I will dwindle for a second time*
*shrink again to insignificance*
*my legs mere spindles*
            *my boots gape and flap*
*the walk into town grows longer*
*my fingers tremble the coins in my purse*
*I'm becoming the sort of woman who*
*dithers in post office queues.*
*So I'll dream on the coastal footpaths*
            *till the treacherous footing, the cloying mud*
*threaten to curb all my courage.*
            *I will walk instead along fields full of stubble*
*counting the skylarks – listen to them dwindle.*

# AFTER EMILY

I stepped away – the Cliff's sore Lip –
was cracked and trembling there
It leered at me salaciously
And seemed to cry – Beware

The buzzing Thoughts of Suicides
Still pollinate the Rim
So did the Bride Groom's winning Smile
Despite a View – so grim

The Wind has Ammunition rare –
Delirium contrives –
White Birds like Michelangelo
Carved Beauty from the Skies

The Sea was Sapphire – Ruby Sun
It blinked in to Eclipse –
The Soul has moments of Despair
Then sinks into Abyss

# AS IF FROM NOWHERE

Is there nothing left to touch us, but the hands of the past
that fumble for our feet as we tread the cliff paths?

Is there nothing else to feel except the seasons' flow
as we watch for the sun's dying afterglow?

Time is like the tide as it creeps towards the dunes
we are grains of sand – abrading – deaf to its tunes.

There are only so many songs to be sung,
only the singer can give it new tongue,

but singular though that voice may seem,
it echoes the murmur of pebbles in the stream...

And then, as if from nowhere,
        resting on an updraft,
                a single gull soars above
                        the cliff's hidden face.

# SURFERS AND JUMPERS

From the top of the cliff they look like seals –
    sleek
            wet-suited bodies gleaming in grey waves

their cheeks resting on their boards as they loll –
    waiting
            lazily nonchalant, they rise and fall

                rise and fall.

She's watching them from the top of the cliff
    dreaming
            of updrafts, of gulls, she raises her arms

her pulse speaking to the throb of the tide
    she seeks
            safer footing behind her – rise and fall

                leap and fall.

# ON EDGE

Like iron filings on a hidden magnet
my errant feet are drawn by fear.
Others, carefree stride this path:
joggers, runners in high-tech shoes,
couples who loiter, out-facing the wind,
parents with laughing children on their shoulders,
or loners whose eyes reflect only the clouds.

Once I walked backwards over this edge,
here where rock samphire clings,
its succulent fingers to be licked for the salt.
You have time to notice such things
when abseiling – and the day-moths
that brush your face with dust
as they sip the sweat from your cheeks.

Do the jumpers, the sad ones, face forward,
hovering on the brink,
their eyes upon the horizon?
Maybe there's something joyous in that leap,
arms wide open to sea and sky;
stepping out over nothingness,
leaving guilt as a parting gift.

After the head-swoon over the lip
descent is surprisingly easy.
Safe in the harness, right hand on the rope,
tempted to ricochet off the rock face,
I bounce with such smug satisfaction.
I am a spider-woman – all in one piece
when finally my feet touch the beach.

# STILL LIFE?

After a great tumult
perhaps a cliff fall
there is such a stillness – as if the echo
of its roar had been swallowed whole.

Some malevolent conjuror
has surely been at work:
the whirling ammonites' dance
now frozen;
devils' toenails, swept up then bundled,
claw through a layer
of petrified mud.
Rocks, the size of dinosaur eggs,
reel eternally
in limestone cavities.

Out at sea
Nash Sands shows its back,
breaching like a whale.

Tusker rock rises, crusted with wrecks:
the boiler from a dredger
and its propeller, a crankshaft
engine block, steel plates from a hull;
barque, brig and schooner,
smack, sloop or snow;
names now scoured of meaning.

Today the cliffs merely
threaten to fall,
re-join the boulders
encumbering this beach;
stone life as still life
in muted hues.

I pick my way among washed-up
things.

Where are the birds?

# SHEER DISBELIEF

'Who made that, then?' said the child, as we walked along the shore.
'What?'
'That', he replied, pointing at the cliffs.
'Er, God.'
'Nah. Come on. Really, what they for? Who built them?'
I tried to explain Time; sedimentation, the limestone platforms on which we walked.
'Nah. What they *for?*' he said.

# ACKNOWLEDGEMENTS

The Owl was published in *Trestle Ties* Issue One Winter/Spring 2019

Scribble (with the title, Arthritis) was published in *The Cabinet of Heed* Issue 4

Toads was published in *The Cabinet of Heed Issue* 14

Bird Watching and All Saints Day were published in *The Lonely Crowd* Issue 10

Grounded was published in *The Broken Spine Artist Collective*: Third Edition

A version of Last Pickings called Dad's Plot was published in *The New Welsh Review* February 2021

Surfers and Jumpers was published in *Black Bough* Issue 4 Divine Darkness

The following poems have been published on line for *Black Bough* Poems #TopTweetTuesday:

Purple, Once upon an April, November, Dung Spiders, A Man with a Gun, Sheer Disbelief, Still Life and Snowdrop.

I would like to thank Dr Jasmine Donahaye of Swansea University's Creative Writing Department for her help, encouragement, advice and unfailing eye for detail.

Ticking is dedicated to the memory of Welsh poet, Nigel Jenkins who first inspired me to write poetry.